Anonymous

An Act for the Relief and Release of Poor Distressed Prisoners for Debt or Dammages

Anonymous

An Act for the Relief and Release of Poor Distressed Prisoners for Debt or Dammages

ISBN/EAN: 9783337148775

Printed in Europe, USA, Canada, Australia, Japan

Cover: Foto ©ninafisch / pixelio.de

More available books at **www.hansebooks.com**

AN
ACT
FOR THE
Relief and Releaſe
Of Poor Diſtreſſed
PRISONERS
FOR
Debt or Dammages.

DUBLIN:
Printed by *Andrew Crook*, Printer to the King's Moſt *Excellent* Majeſty, on the *Blind-Key*, near *Copper-Alley*, *M. DC. XC. IX.*

An ACT for the Relief and Release of poor Distressed Prisoners for Debt or Dammages.

CHAP. I.

FORASMUCH as very many persons now detained in Prison, are miserably Impoverished, either by reason of the late Unhappy Rebellion in this Kingdom, their own Misfortunes, or otherwise, so as they are totally Disabled to give any Satisfaction to their Creditors; and by being detained in Prison without advantage to any, are rendered Useless and a Burthen to the Kingdom, to the great Prejudice thereof.

Be it therefore Enacted by the Kings Most Excellent Majesty, by, and with the Advice and Consent of the Lords Spiritual and Temporal, and Commons in this present Parliament Assembled, and by Authority of the same, That all persons who were in Prison upon the First Day of August, in the Year of Our Lord God One thousand Six hundred Ninety seaven, for Debt or Damages, or for, or upon any Action or Actions, or upon any Mean Process for Debt, or other Actions whatsoever; which Actions by Prosecution of Law may become Judgments, or who have Judgments Entred upon Record against them, or are Charged in Execution, or Imprisoned

Imprisoned upon Attachment Debt, or upon Outlawries, before or after Judgment for Debt, or upon any other Process whatsoever, Issuing out of any Court of Law or Equity, for the Cause of Debt or Damages, or Costs only, who shall take the Oath hereafter mentioned, shall and may be Released, and Discharged from their Imprisonment, in such way and manner, as is herein and hereafter provided.

And be it further Enacted by the Authority aforesaid, That it shall and may be lawful to, and for any Justice of the Peace of any County, City, Town or Liberty, within the Kingdom of Ireland, by Warrant under his Hand and Seal, to Require the Sheriff, Goaler, or Keeper of any Prison within his respective Jurisdiction, to bring before him without delay, the Body of any Person being in Prison for Debt, or any other Action, as aforesaid, on the First Day of August aforesaid, and the said person Petitioning such Justice to be Discharged to some convenient place, within the distance of One Mile from the said Prison, and shall certifie the Cause and Causes of the Imprisonment, before the same Justice; which Warrant every such Sheriff, Goaler and Keeper, is hereby Commanded to obey: And in Case such Prisoner coming before such Justice, shall take an Oath to this effect, before the said Justice.

I A. B. do upon my Corporal Oath, Solemnly Profess and Declare before Almighty God, That I am not worth in Lands, Money, Goods or Stock, nor any other Estate, Real or Personal in Possession, Reversion, or Remainder, of the value of Five pounds in the whole, or sufficient to pay the

the Debt or Damage, for which I am Impriſoned: And that I have not directly, or indirectly Sold, Leaſed, or otherwiſe Conveyed, Diſpoſed of, or Intruſted all, or any part of my ſaid Money, Lands, Goods, Stock, or Eſtate, whereby to ſecure the ſame to Receive, or expect any profit or advantage thereof, or to Defraud or Deceive any Creditor or Creditors whatſoever, to whom I am Indebted.

So help me God, &c.

Which ſaid Oath, the ſaid Juſtice of the Peace, is hereby Impowered and Authorized to Adminiſter; that then after the making of ſuch Oath, the ſaid Juſtice ſhall Remand the Priſoner to Priſon, and ſhall without Fee give a Certificate thereof in Writing under his Hand and Seal, to the ſaid Priſoner, to be ſerved on ſuch perſon or perſons, his or their Executors, or Adminiſtrators, or to be left at the place of the uſual Abode of ſuch perſon or perſons, at whoſe Sute the Priſoner ſtandeth Charged and Impriſoned, thereby appointing as well the ſaid perſon or perſons, as the ſaid Priſoner, to appear before the Juſtices at the next General-Quarter-Seſſions of the Peace, to be held for the ſame County, City, Town or Liberty; and when it ſhall appear upon Oath, before the ſaid Juſtices, which ſaid Oath, the ſaid Juſtices are hereby Impowered and Authorized to Adminiſter, that the ſaid Certificate was ſo ſerved, or left, Ten Days or more, before the ſaid Seſſions; and that the ſaid Oath taken by the ſaid Priſoner, be not diſproved by good Teſtimony, of any Credible perſon or perſons upon Oath, to be Adminiſtred by the ſaid Juſtices, by Vertue of this Act; Then the ſaid Juſtices being satisfied therein, shall without Fee direct their Warrant under their Hands and Seals, commanding the said Sheriff, Goaler, or Keeper of the Prison, to let at Liberty, and Discharge the said Prisoner, if Imprisoned for the Causes aforesaid, and no other, without paying any thing for the Fees, or Chamber-Rent; Which Warrant shall be a sufficient Discharge to the said Sheriff, Goaler, or Keeper of the Prison, and no Action of Escape, or other Action shall be brought against them, or any of them in any Wise for the same.

Provided always, That if any Creditor shall insist to have his Debtor continued in Prison after he hath taken the said Oath, and will allow him a Weekly Maintainance, to be appointed by the Justices of the Peace, not exceeding Fourteen pence the Week; that such Prisoner shall be continued in Prison for the space of Three Months, on Payment of the said Weekly Allowance, as aforesaid; which said Money shall be Paid Weekly to the said Prisoner himself, and not to the Goaler, Keeper, or any other for him: And if within the space of Three Months, after such Weekly Allowance by any Creditor, no Estate of the Prisoner shall be Discovered or Made out, before Two Justices of the Peace of that County and Division, where the said Prisoner is kept in Prison, then the said Prisoner shall without Fee be forthwith Discharged, by Warrant under the Hands and Seals of any Two Justices of the Peace, of the same County or Division, where the said Prisoner shall be so Imprisoned, to the Keeper of such Prison, in that behalf Directed as fully and amply, as if such Prisoner shall be so Imprisoned to the

Keeper

Keeper of such Prison in that behalf, directed as fully and amply as if such Prisoner had been Discharged by Justices of the Peace at the Quarter-Sessions: And that then, and from thenceforth, the said Weekly Allowance shall cease and determine, as if the same had never been made.

And be it further Enacted by the Authority aforesaid, That no Prisoner Discharged out of Prison by Virtue of this present Act, shall at any time hereafter be Imprisoned for, or by reason of any Debt or Damages, or any Summ or Summs of Money contracted or grown due to, or recovered by any person or persons at whose Sute the said Prisoner did stand Charged in any Prison, or any other person or persons to whom such Prisoner did give notice under the Hand and Seal of some Justice of the Peace of the same County or place, the space of Ten days before the time of his Discharge, of his Intention to receive the Benefit of this Act, and of the Way and Course he intended to take for obtaining the same, before the time of their Discharge, as aforesaid. But that upon any Arrest for such Debt, Damages, or Summs of Money, it shall and may be Lawful for them, shewing a Duplicate of their Discharges under the Hands and Seals of the Justices of the Peace, by whom they were Discharged, or of any Two of them, or of such Justices of the Peace, in Case such Prisoner be discharged after an Allowance of Maintenance by the Creditors for Three Months, as aforesaid, which the said Justices are hereby Required to give without Fee to every Prisoner so by them discharged, to retain an Attorney to appear for them, and File Common Bail to every such

Action

Action and Plead thereunto, so that the Plantiff (if he please) may Recover and Enter Judgment against such Prisoner, to be Executed and Levyed upon the Lands Tenements, Goods and Chattels of such Prisoner so discharged, as aforesaid; his or her Wareing Apparel, Furniture for his or her Dwelling House, the said Furniture and Necessary Tools for his or her Trade and Occupation not exceeding Five pounds in Value, only Excepted, but not upon the person or persons of the Prisoners, the persons of such Prisoners being hereby for ever freed and discharged from Imprisonment for any Debt, Trespass upon the Case, Duty, Summ or Summs of Money, or things thereunto relating, contracted or due before the time of their Discharge, having had Notice, as aforesaid.

And be it further Enacted by the Authority aforesaid, That in Case any Sheriff, Goaler, or Keeper of a Prison, shall refuse or delay for Three days, to bring before such Justice of the Peace, or after a Warrant of Discharge delivered to him, as aforesaid, refuse or neglect to set at Liberty any Prisoner or Prisoners according to the said Order of the Justice or Justices of the Peace, made in the pursuance of this Act; every such Goaler, Sheriff, or Keeper of Prison shall Forfeit and pay to such Prisoner so detained, contrary to such Order, the Summ of Twenty pounds, to be Recovered by Bill, Plaint, Sute, or Action of Debt, in any of His Majesty's Courts of Record, wherein no Essoyne Protection, or Wager of Law is to be allowed, nor more than one Imparlance Granted; and shall also be liable and subject to such

Fine

Fine and Imprisonment for such time, not exceeding Two Months, as the said Justices of the Peace shall, upon Complaint thereof to them made, Order and Award.

And be it further Enacted by the Authority aforesaid, That upon any Action of Escape, or other Sute brought, or to be brought, against any Justice of the Peace, Sheriff, Goaler, or Keeper of Prison, for any thing done in Obedience to this Act, it shall and may be Lawful to, and for any such Justice of the Peace, Sheriff, Goaler, and Keeper of Prison, to Plead the General Issue, and give this Act in Evidence, which shall be a Good and Sufficient Discharge, and save harmless every such Justice of the Peace, Sheriff, Goaler and Keeper of Prison, Pleading the same; and if the Plantiff in any such Action be Non-Suted, or Verdict pass against him, the Defendant shall have Double Costs, to be Taxed by the Court where such Action is brought.

Provided always, That the Discharge of any person or persons by Virtue of this Act, shall not amount unto, or be construed to Free or Discharge any other person or persons joyntly or severally Bound for, or lyable to Answer or Satisfy the said Debt, or any part thereof, either as Principal or Surety, but that such other person or persons shall be lyable to Answer the said Debt and Damages in such manner, to all Intents and purposes, as they were before the Discharge of such prisoner.

Provided also, That no person by Virtue of this Act, shall be discharged out of prison who shall be Charged in Execution with more than the Summ of Fifty pounds to any one person principal Money and Damages.

Provided always, That if any prisoner who shall be released by Virtue of this Act, shall at any time afterwards be found, or suspected by any Creditor to have in ready Money, Goods or Chattels in his own hands and possession, or in the hands of any others to his or her use, or in Trust for him or her, in Value over and above what he or she is allowed by this Act, other than such Goods in his Shop or Work-House, as he shall have been Credited and Trusted with since the time of his Discharge, and for what he shall be really Indebted at the time of making such Oath, and he or she will not, or do not upon Covenient demand, pay his or her Debt or Debts therewith, as far as the same will reach, that then, and in such Case, at the request of any Creditor, the said Oath shall be tendered to him or her again by any Justice of the Peace in this Act before Impowered to Administer the said Oath for Discharge of Prisoners, or by any Judge of the Court wherein there is Judgment against him when he or she refusing to take the said Oath, shall be Remanded to prison, in Execution for such Debt or Debts, any thing in this Act to the contrary, Notwithstanding.

Provided also, That this Act shall not extend to any person or persons in Execution for any Fine on him or her Imposed for any Offence by him or her committed.

Provided, that such person or persons as is, or are detained in Prison upon any Measne Process, if it shall be desired by any

any Creditor before any Justice of the Peace, to whom such Prisoner has applyed for his Discharge, shall forthwith give a Warrant to some Attorney to appear, or File common Bail for him, or them, in the Court out of which the said Measne Process issued, and to receive a Declaration at the Plantiffs Sute; and that such Prisoner shall thereupon have the full Benefit of this Law, as to the Liberty of his person, against his said Imprisonment, upon the said Measne Process, and against any Judgment, or Execution, that shall be had against him in that Sute, and against any other Sute that shall be brought against him for the same matter, or cause of Action, to all intents and purposes as fully and beneficially, as if he had been charged in Execution at the said Plantiffs Sute, before the First Day of August aforesaid; but such person in Prison upon Measne Process, shall in case of his refusal to give such Warrant of Attorney, loose the whole Benefit of this Act.

Provided always, That no Merchant Stranger, or other Alien or Foreigner, that hath been Arrested, and is in Prison on any Action or Sute, for, or by reason of any Debt, or other Engagement contracted, or Entred into beyond the Seas, shall have any Benefit of this Act; but that all, and every such Merchant Stranger, and other Alien and Foreigner, shall, and may be detained in prison, and proceeded against as if this Act had never been made.

Provided always, That no prisoner shall be Discharged by Virtue of this Act, until he shall before the Justices of Peace, who are by this Act impowered to Discharge him, declare upon his, or her Corporal Oath, which Oath the

the said Justices are hereby appointed to Administer, what Effects are belonging to him or her, and what Debt or Debts are then Owing to him or her, within any His Majesty's Dominions, or elsewhere, and by whom, and for what Cause, and upon what Security; of all which a Schedule shall be made in the presence of such Justices, and Subscribed by the Prisoner, and shall be by such Justices returned to the next Quarter-Sessions, there to be kept for the better Information of the Creditor of such Prisoner, who, or such of them as will joyn, may thereupon Sue for such Debts, or so much thereof, as will reasonably satisfie them, in the Name of the Prisoner; and after the same Recovered and Received, to render the Over-plus thereof (their own Debts and Charges first Deducted) to the Prisoner.

Provided always, and to Deterr all persons who are by the Charitable Intention of this Act to be Relieved, from abusing the Favour hereby to them intended.

Be it Enacted, That if any person who shall in pursuance of this Act, take his Oath for any the purposes hereby appointed, shall Forswear, or Perjure him or herself, then such person being Lawfully Convicted thereof, shall beyond, and over and above the Penalties which may by the Law now in being inflicted, Suffer Imprisonment for the space of Seaven Years, without Bail or Mainprize.

FINIS.

AN

ACT

For Reforming

ABUSES

In Making of

Butter-Cask,

And Preventing Falſe packing of

BUTTER.

DUBLIN:
Printed by *Andrew Crook*, Printer to the King's Moſt *Excellent* Majeſty, on the *Blind-Key*, near *Copper-Alley*, *M. DC. XC. IX.*

An ACT for Reforming Abuses in Making of Butter-Cask, and Preventing of false Packing of Butter.

CHAP. II.

FORASMUCH as Butter is one of the principal Commodities of the Product of this Kingdom, and is not only of an Universal Use and Expence at Home, but very great Quantities thereof are Transported beyond the Seas.

And whereas by Custom, every Barrel of Butter ought to weigh Two hundred Sixty four pounds Gross, at the least; That is to say, Two hundred Twenty four pounds of Neat Butter, and the Cask not to exceed in Weight Forty pounds. Every Three Quarter Barrel ought to weigh, One hundred Ninety eight pounds Gross, (viz.) One hundred Sixty eight pounds, of good and Merchantable Butter, Neat, and the Cask not to exceed in Weight, Thirty pounds. Every half Barrel of Butter ought to weigh, One hundred Thirty two pounds (viz.) One hundred and Twelve pounds, of good and Merchantable Butter, Neat, and the Cask not to exceed in weight Twenty pounds. And every Firkin of Butter ought to weigh Sixty six pounds (viz.) Fifty six pounds of of good and Merchantable Butter, Neat, and the Cask not to exceed Ten pounds.

And, Whereas great Complaint hath been made by the Merchants, and Traders in Butter, That by the Fraudulent Dealing and practices of Coopers, in making the Cask for Package of Butter, of Unseasoned Timber, and of several Farmers, Owners and Packers of Butter, who by their Irregular manner of Weighing with Stones, and other Unwarrantable Weights, and Packing their Butter in Cask Weighing more than they ought to do, not only being a great Dishonour to this Nation, in the Parts beyond the Seas, but also the said Commodity is brought in great Dis-repute abroad, whereby it Yields not that Price, nor is Vended there in such Quantities as otherwise it would. For prevention whereof, May it please Your Majesty that it may be Enacted.

And be it Enacted by the King's Most Excellent Majesty, by, and with the Advice and Consent of the Lords Spiritual and Temporal, and Commons in this present Parliament Assembled, and by the Authority of the same, That from and after the Twenty fifth Day of March, which will be in the Year of Our Lord God One thousand Six hundred Ninety eight, no Cooper, nor other person whatsoever in this Kingdom of Ireland, shall hereafter at any time, presume to make, or Cause to be made, any Butter-Cask whatsoever for Sale, but such only as shall be made of sound Dry and well Seasoned Timber, according to the several Gages and Weights herein-after mentioned, and known by the several Names following,

lowing (That is to say) The Firkin, Half-Barrel, Three Quarter Barrels, and Barrel, And that every Firkin do, and shall contain Two Quarters of an hundred, at Five Score and Twelve pounds to the Hundred, Neat, besides the Tare of the Cask, and not less, of good and Merchantable Butter, and that Cask not to weigh above Ten pounds, and to contain and hold Seaven Gallons: And every Half Barrel do, and shall contain One hundred weight, Neat, at Five Score and Twelve pounds to the Hundred, and not less, of good and Merchantable Butter, besides the Weight of the Cask, and the Cask not to weigh above Twenty pounds, and to measure Fourteen Gallons: Every Three Quarter Barrel do, and shall contain One hundred and Two Quarters, Neat, at Five Score and Twelve pounds to the Hundred, besides the weight of the Cask, and not less, of Good and Merchantable Butter, and the Cask not to weigh above Thirty pounds, and to measure Twenty one Gallons: And every Barrel do, and shall contain Two hundred weight Neat, at Five Score and Twelve pounds to the Hundred, besides the Weight of the Cask, and not less, of Good and Merchantable Butter, and the Cask not to weigh above Forty pounds, and to measure Twenty eight Gallons. And that every such Cask, hereafter to be made, shall be made with Three Hoops on each Quarter, to be set on with Twigs, or sufficiently Notched, and have Two Heads to be put into Riggles, and made tight, so as to hold Pickle, and that no Cap Heads be hereafter made for any such Cask to be Exposed

to

to Sale as aforesaid. And for the better discovery of all Frauds or Abuses which shall be committed against this Act,

Be it further Enacted by the Authority aforesaid, That every Cooper, or other person making Cask for putting Butter in, as aforesaid, shall set upon every Firkin, Half-Barrel, Three Quarter Barrel, and Barrel so made of Seasoned Timber, as aforesaid, a Mark, with the first Letter of his and their Christian Name, and his and their Sirname at length, with an Iron Brand, with a Mark for the City, Town, Village, or Parish wherein he lives; and that every Farmer and other person or persons hereafter at any time Packing up Butter, or Exposing the same to Sale, shall from and after the said Twenty fifth Day of March One thousand Six hundred Ninety eight, Pack up his Butter in such Sufficient Cask, made of Sound, Dry, and Well-Seasoned Timber, and Marked as aforesaid, and in none other, and shall set upon every such Firkin and Cask, when the same is fully and throughly Seasoned, by filling such Cask with Water, and not to be put standing in Water; and when the same is filled with Butter, the first Letter of his and their Christian Name, and his and their Sirname at length, with an Iron Brand; and if the said Cooper or Farmer, or other person or persons whatsoever making Cask, or Packing up Butter, or Exposing the same to Sale, as aforesaid, shall at any time from and after the said Twenty fifth day of March One thousand Six hundred Ninety eight, offend, by omitting to do what he or they are Required by this Act to do and perform, he or

they

they so Offending, and being Convicted upon Oath of the said Offence, before one or more of His Majesties Justices of the Peace, or Chief Magistrate of any Corporation, by one or more Witness or Witnesses, which Oath the said Justice or Justices, or Chief Magistrate are hereby Impowered, and are Required to Administer, or upon Confession of the Offender or Offenders before such Justice or Justices, or Chief Magistrate, the said party or parties so Offending, shall Forfeit for every such Offence, to the Use of the Poor of the Parish where such Offence shall be committed, the Summ of Ten Shillings, for every Hundred Weight of Butter, and so proportionably for every greater or lesser Quantity that shall be in every such Cask, to be Levyed by Distress and Sale of the Offenders Goods and Chattels, the Over-plus to be restored, after all Charges of the said Distress defrayed: And every Constable of the Parish, or chief Constable of the Barony where such Offence shall be committed, are hereby Authorized and Required to Levy the same accordingly by Warrant under the Hand and Seal of such Justice or Justices, or Chief Magistrate, so to do; and in Case such Offender or Offenders shall not have Goods and Chattels sufficient for the Levying the said Penalty, that then it shall and may be Lawful for the Justice or Justices, or Chief Magistrate before whom such Conviction shall be made, by Warrant under their Hand and Seal, to appoint such Offender or Offenders to be publickly Set in the Stocks for the space of Two hours.

And be it further Enacted by the Authority aforesaid, That all Goods and Merchandizes of the

the Growth and Manufactury of this Kingdom, usually sold by the Hundred Weight, shall from and after the said Twenty fifth day of March One thousand Six hundred Ninety eight, be Bought and Sold at Five Score and Twelve pounds to the Hundred Weight, and no more, upon pain of Forfeiture of the Summ of Ten Shillings, for Buying and Selling any Goods and Merchandizes contrary to the true Intent and Meaning of this Act.

And be it further Enacted by the Authority aforesaid, That if any Action or Sute shall be commenced or brought against any Justice or Justices of the Peace, or Chief Magistrate, Constable or other person whatsoever, for doing or causing to be done, any thing in pursuance of this Act concerning the said Offences; the Defendant or Defendants in such Action, shall, and may plead the General Issue, and give the special matter in Evidence; And if upon such Action, Verdict be given for the Defendant or Defendants, or if the Plantiff become Non-sute, or Dis-continue his Action, then the Defendant or Defendants, shall have Treble Costs.

Provided always, and it is hereby Enacted by the Authority aforesaid, That no person shall be Prosecuted or Troubled for any Offence done against this Statute, unless the same be Proved or Prosecuted within the space of Three Months next after the Offence committed.

And whereas in an Act passed this present Session of Parliament, Intituled, An Act for Granting an Additional Duty on Tobacco, and for continuing unto His Majesty an Aid or Additional Custom on several Goods and Merchandizes; and

and also for continuing the Additional Duty on Beer and Ale, and other Liquors, till the Twenty fifth of *December*, One thousand Seaven hundred and Two, it is among other things Enacted as follows; That is to say,

Be it further Enacted by the Authority aforesaid, That all Tobacco, Muslin, Callicoes, and all sorts of Linnen, Scotch Cloath, and Wines, except Wines of the growth of Spain, and of the Dominions thereunto belonging, that shall be Imported into this Kingdom at any time, from and after the Four and twentieth Day of December, One thousand Six hundred Ninety nine, unto the Five and twentieth of December, which shall be in the Year, One Seaven hundred and Two, and no longer, shall Answer and Pay unto His Majesty, His Heirs and Successors, over and above all Rates and Duties Due, or Payable, for, or out of the same, by Vertue of any former, or other Law in this Kingdom, &c. In which Clause, the word Thousand is omitted, after the word One, and before the words Seaven hundred and Two, whereby some Doubt may hereafter arise; Whether the said Duties on Tobacco, Muslin, Callicoes, Linnen, Scotch-Cloath, and Wines, Imported after the Twenty fourth of December, One thousand Six hundred Ninety nine, unto the Twenty fifth of December, One thousand Seaven hundred and Two, may be Demanded, or ought to be Received. For the Removing therefore of the said Doubt, and Explaining the said Act in that particular,

Be it Declared and Enacted by the Authority aforesaid, That the said Act shall at all times hereafter, be Construed and Taken in the same, and no other Sence or Meaning, then as if the Word Thousand had not been Omitted, between the Words before mentioned; and that the Duties, and Additional Duties, by the said before Recited Act, intended to be Granted for, and out of Tobacco, Muslin, Callicoes, Linnen, Scotch-Cloath, and Wines, aforesaid, Imported into this Kingdom, from the Twenty fourth of December One thousand Six hundred Ninety nine, shall be Demandable by, and Payable to His Majesty out of all such Goods and Commodities to be Imported into this Kingdom, from the said Twenty fourth of December One thousand Six hundred Ninety nine, to the twenty fifth of December One thousand Seaven hundred and two, and no longer, in the same manner as if the Word Thousand had not been omitted in the said former Act, but the same had been in the following Words, One thousand Seaven hundred and Two.

FINIS.

AN

A C T

FOR

Determining Differences

BY

ARBITRATION.

AN

A C T

For the better

Management and Dispoſal

OF THE

L A N D S

Set a part for the Support of the

Fort of Duncanon.

DUBLIN: Printed by *Andrew Crook*, Printer to the King's Moſt Excellent Majeſty, on the *Blind-Key*, near *Copper-Alley*, MDCXCXC.

An ACT for Determining Differences by Arbitration.

CHAP. XIV.

WHEREAS it hath been found by Experience, that References made by Rule of Court, hath Contributed much to the ease of the Subject, in Determining of Controversies, because the parties become thereby oblidged to perform the Award of Arbitrators Chosen by themselves, under the Penalty of Imprisonment for their Contempt, in Case they refuse to perform the same.

Now for promoting Trade, and rendring the Awards of Arbitrators the more effectual in all Cases, for the final Determination of Controversies Referred to them by Merchants and Traders or others, containing Matters of Account or Trade, or other Matters.

Be it Enacted by the King's most Excellent Majesty, by, and with the Advice and Consent of the Lords Spiritual and Temporal, and Commons in this present Parliament Assembled, and by Authority of the same; That from and after the First day of March, which shall be in the year of Our Lord, One thousand Six hundred

hundred Ninety eight, it may be lawful for all Merchants, Traders and others, desiring to end by Arbitration, any Controversie, Sute or Quarrel; Controversies, Sutes or Quarrels, for which there is no other Remedy but by personal Action or Sute in Equity to Agree, that their Submission of the Matter to the Award or Umpirage of any person or persons, should be made a Rule of any of His Majesty's Courts of Record, which the parties shall choose, and to Insert such their Agreement in their Submission, or the Condition of the Bond or Promise, Whereby they oblidge themselves respectively, to submit to the Award or Umpirage of any person or persons: Which Agreement being so made, and Inserted in their Submission or Promise, or Condition of their respective Bonds, shall or may upon producing an Affidavit thereof, made by the Witnesses thereunto, or any one of them, in the Court of which the same is Agreed to be made a Rule, and reading and fileing the said Affidavit in Court, be Entred of Record in such Court, and a Rule shall be thereupon made by the said Court, that the parties shall submit to, and Finally be concluded by the Arbitration or Umpirage, which shall be made by the Arbitrators or Umpire, pursuant to such Submission; and in Case of Disobedience to such Arbitation or Umpirage, the party neglecting or refusing to perform or Execute the same, or any part thereof, shall be Subject to all the penalties by the Course and Practise of such Court, usuall inflicted on such as Contemn a Rule of the said Court, made in a Cause depending therein; and the Court on Motion shall Issue Process accordingly; which Process shall

not

not be stopt or delayed in its Execution, by any Order, Rule, Command or Process of any other Court, either of Law or Equity, unless it shall be made appear on Oath to such Court, that the Arbitrators or Umpire Mis-behaved themselves, and that such Award, Arbitration or Umpirage, was procured by Corruption or other undue Means.

And be it further Enacted by the Authority aforesaid, That any Arbitration or Umpirage procured by Corruption or undue Means, shall be Judged and Esteémed void and of none effect, and accordingly be set aside by any Court of Law or Equity; so as Complaint of such Corruption or undue Practise, be made in the Court, where the Rule is made for Submission to such Arbitration or Umpirage before the last Day of the next Term after such Arbitration or Umpirage made and published to the parties; any thing herein contained to the contrary notwithstanding.

An ACT for the better Mannagement and Disposal of the Lands set apart for the Support of the Fort of *Duncannon*.

CHAP. XV.

Whereas in and by one Act Intituled, An Act for the better Execution of His Majesty's Gracious Declaration, for the Settlement of His Majesty's Kingdom of *Ireland*, and satisfaction of the several Interests of Adventurers, Soldiers, and other His Subjects there. It is among other things Enacted and Provided to the effect following.

 That

That the Commissioners for Execution of the said Act, should set out or cause to be set out, so much of the Forfeited Lands, as do amount unto the clear yearly value of Three hundred pounds per annum, and are nearest adjacent, and lye most contiguous unto the Fort of Duncannon; which Lands so as aforesaid, to be set out shall be reserved unto His Majesty, his Heirs and Successors, to the intent, that the Rents, Issues and Profits thereof, may for ever be Imployed for, and towards the better Support and Maintenance of the Fort aforesaid; and all and every the Adventurers and Soldiers, and other reprisable persons, to whom any of the said Lands, so as aforesaid to be set out, have been heretofore Allotted o Disposed, shall be forthwith Reprised out of some other Forfeited Lands, of an Estate of equal value, worth and purchase; any thing in the said Act contained to the contrary notwithstanding.

And whereas in Pursuance and Execution of the said Clause in the said Act; the said Commissioners have set out the several Forfeited Lands hereafter mentioned: That is to say, the Lands of Knockroe, and passage, containing One hundred Fifty nine Acres, Crooke, Two hundred Seventy five Acres, Newtowne, containing Two hundred Sixty six Acres, Knocknegaple, containing Eighty two Acres, Rahin, containing Ninety four Acres; and in Fatlegg, which were Retrenched by Captain Bolton, Two hundred Seventy two Acres, in the Barony of Gualtire, in the County of Waterford, or County of the City of Waterford, and reserved the same unto His late Majesty King Charles the Second, for the Fulfilling and

An-

Answering the Intents and Purposes aforesaid. And His said late Majesty hath by Letters Patents, bearing Date the One and twentieth day of May, in the One and twentieth Year of His said late Majesty's Reign, Granted the same unto Richard Earl of Arran, Marcus Lord Viscount Dungannon, Sir John Temple, Knight, then Master of the Rolls of this Kingdom, Sir Robert Byrone, and Sir Theophilus Jones, and the Heirs of the Survivor of them in Trust, for, and to Answer the Uses, Intents and Purposes, aforesaid; and not any way for the Use, Benefit or Behoof of the said Patentees, or any of them, or any of their Heirs.

And Whereas the Right Honourable Richard late Earl of Arran, one of the said Patentees, Survived all and every the said other Patentees, and became Seized of all and every the said Lands by Survivorship, to the Uses, Intents and Purposes aforesaid; and the same after the Decease of the said Earl, are Descended upon the Honourable the Lady Charlote Butler, only Daughter and Heiress of the said Earl, through whose Minority, and usual Residence and Abode in England, the said Trusts and Purposes cannot be Performed, Executed or Discharged, as the publick Service Requires; and thereby the said Fort cannot be so Supported and Repaired, nor the said Estate mannaged to the best Advantage: To Answer the Ends aforesaid,

Be it therefore Enacted by the King's most Excellent Majesty, by, and with the Advice and Consent of the Lords Spiritual and Temporal and Commons in Parliament Assembled, and by Authority of the same; That the said Lands, and all the Estate, Right, Title and Interest,

Interest, in, and to the said Towns and Lands abovementioned, which came and Descended to the said Lady Charlote Butler, Daughter and Heiress to the said Richard Earl of Arran, shall be, and hereby is and are Vested and Adjudged to be Vested in Phillip Savage Esquire, Thomas Brodrick Esquire, Colonel William Ponsonby, Sir John Mason and Allan Brodrick Esquire, their Heirs and Assigns, in the same manner to all intents, as the same before passing this Act were, in the said Lady Charlote Butler; and that the said Phillip Savage, Thomas Brodrick, William Ponsonby, Sir John Mason, and Allan Brodrick, their Heirs and Assigns, shall Stand and be Seized thereof, to the same Trusts, Intents and Purposes, as the said Charlote Butler stood Seized thereof, by, from and after the Decease of her said Father, and to no other Use, Trust or Purpose whatsoever.

Saving to all persons whatsoever; and to all Bodies Politick and Corporate, all such Possession, Estate, Right, Title, Claim, Demand, Entry, Action or cause of Action whatsoever, in Law or Equity, as the said persons had, or might have had, if this present Act had not been made.

FINIS.

AN

A C T

For the more

EASY,

AND

Speedy Securing,

AND

RECOVERY

OF

SMALL DEBTS.

DUBLIN:
Printed by *Andrew Crook*, Printer to the King's Most Excellent Majesty, on *Cork-Hill*, near *Copper-Alley*. M DC XC VII.

An ACT for the more Easie, and Speedy Securing, and Recovery of Small Debts.

CHAP. LX.

WHEREAS nothing would conduce more to the Advancement of Trade, Commerce, and Industry in this Kingdom, then that an Easie, and Summary Way, for the Recovery, and Securing of Small Debts, might be found, Whereby an Universal Credit, might be Established among the Trading people of this Realm, without the necessity of Tedious, and Costly Sutes of Law. May it therefore please your Majesty, that it may be Enacted.

And be it Enacted by the King's Most Excellent Majesty; by, and with the Advice and Consent of the Lords Spiritual and Temporal, and Commons in this present Parliament Assembled, and by Authority of the same; That in every County, and every County of a City, and County of a Town, in this Kingdom of Ireland; some person before the First Day of February, in this present year of Our Lord, One thousand Six hundred Ninety seaven, be appointed by His Majesty, or by the Lord Lieutenant, Lord Deputy, Lord Justice, or Lords Justices, or other Chief Governour or Governours of this Kingdom, for the time being, to be Register

gister in each County, or County of a City, or County of a Town; which said person so Appointed, shall be a Resident, or Inhabitant, for the most part, in such County respectively, wherein he shall be, as herein-after Employed, and shall enter into Recognizance of Five hundred pounds Sterling, before some one of the Judges of either Bench, or Barons of His Majesty's Court of Exchequer, or before the Justices of the Peace, at the next Quarter Sessions, to be holden for the said County, for the due Execution of his Office; Which said Recognizance, shall be Filed of Record, in His Majesty's Court of Exchequer in this Kingdom, some time before the last Day of the Ensuing Term, after such Recognizance shall be acknowledged: And that every such Register, of any such County, as aforesaid, shall, and may, by the Authority of this Act, have Power to Appoint One, or more Deputy, or Deputies, to Officiate under him in such County respectively.

And be it further Enacted by the Authority aforesaid, That every such Register, and Deputy or Deputies, before he, or they, shall take upon him, or them respectively, the Execution of the said Office, shall take the following Oath, before some One, or more of the Justices of the Peace of the said County, or County of a City, or County of a Town, or before the Chief Magistrate of such Town, or Corporation, or his Deputy, where such Register shall keep his Office, (viz.)

I A. B. do Swear, that I will according to the best of my Skill and Cunning, duly and faithfully [redacted] the Office of Register (or Deputy Register) in this County, according to an Act of Parliament, Intituled, **An Act for the more Easy and Speedy Securing, and Recovery of Small Debts**, and that I will not Directly, nor Indirectly, demand, take, or receive any manner of Fee, Reward, or Gratuity, by reason, or Colour of my Office, other then such *Fees* as are allowed by the said Act.

So help me God.

And shall then likewise take the Oaths, and Subscribe the Declaration mentioned and contained in an Act of Parliament, made in England, in the Third Year of the Reign of His present Majesty, and the late Queen Mary, Intituled, An Act for the Abrogating the Oath of Supremacy in *Ireland*, and Appointing other Oaths; Which said Oath of Office, and other Oaths, and Declaration, the said Justice or Justices of the Peace or other Chief Magistrate of such Town or Corporation, or his Deputy, are hereby Authorized, Impowered and Required to Administer. And further, that every such Register, Deputy, or Deputies aforesaid, upon the Pain, Penalty, and Forfeiture of his, or their respective Office or Offices, shall take the aforesaid Oath of Office, and the aforesaid Oaths, and Subscribe the Declaration, at the next Quarter-Sessions, or the next Assizes to be holden for the said County, or County of a City, or County of a Town, which shall first happen in Open Court, between the Hours of Nine and Twelve, in the Morning; which said Oaths respectively, and Declaration, the said Judges of Assize, or Justices of the Peace at their respective Sessions are hereby Authorized, Impowered and Required to Administer.

And be it further Enacted by the Authority aforesaid, That from and after the said First day of February next, every person and persons having any Bond or Bill, under Hand and Seal, for any Summ or Summs of Money, not exceeding Ten pounds, principal Money, which said Bond, or Bill, being acknowledged before any person who is a Justice of the Peace in this Kingdom, or before the Chief Magistrate of any Town Corporate, and such Justice of the Peace, or Chief Magistrate, or his Deputy, Certifying such Acknowledgment, which acknowledgment, every Justice of the Peace of this Kingdom, and every Chief Magistrate of any Town Corporate, or his Deputy, are by the Authority of this Act, Impowered and Required to take, and Certificate under their respective Hands and Seals, to make, and deliver, to the party and parties interested in such Bond, or Bonds, Bill, or Bills, which Certificate and Bond, or Bill, being brought to the Register, or his Deputy, of such County, County of a City, or County of a Town, wherein such person is a Justice of the Peace, or Chief Magistrate of a Town Corporate, or his Deputy, such Register, or his Deputy, or Deputies, or one of them, shall in a Book to be Kept for that purpose, make an Entry of the said Bond, or Bill, and Acknowledgment, at large, as also the Receipts and Trans-

Transfers, thereon endorsed, if any be, and from, and after such Entry, the person or persons who perfected the same, his and their Goods and Chattles personal, shall be thereby Bound and Liable to the said Debt and Interest, from the day of Payment, in like manner, as if the same had been a Judgment at Law.

And to the end there may be no Mistakes or Controversies, for, or concerning the said Bonds, or Bills, in relation to the Wording thereof.

Be it further Enacted by the Authority aforesaid, That all such Bonds or Bills as shall be Registered in pursuance of this Act, shall be Printed and Stamped with His Majesty's Arms, and be in the Form following; That is to say.

KNOW all men by these presents, that of in the County of do Acknowledge my self to stand justly Indebted unto of in the County of in the Full and Just Summ of pounds *Sterling*, to be paid to the said His Executors, Administrators, or Assigns, at, or before the day of to the which payment, I Bind my self, my Heirs, Executors and Administrators; and in default of Payment thereof, I do consent, that Execution shall Issue against my Body, Goods and Chattles personal: Witness my Hand and Seal, this day of

And

And in Case that there be Two or more persons Bound in the said Bond, the said Printed Bond shall be Printed and made so, as to comprehended them, and to Bind them Joyntly, and severally. And to the end, Forged and Counterfeit Bonds, or Bills, may be prevented, and the Subjects of this Land, sufficiently provided with the said Bonds, or Bills so Printed and Stamped, at Easy and Moderate Rates.

Be it Enacted by the Authority aforesaid, That every Register of any County, or County of a City, or County of a Town, shall provide in every Market-Town, within their respective Limits and Precincts, a sufficient quantity of such Blank Bonds, or Bills for Sale, Stamped with the King's Arms, and the name of the County, whereof such person shall be Register. And that no person or persons whatsoever, shall Expose to Sale in any such Market-Town, as aforesaid, any Stamped Printed Bonds, or Bills, other then such as shall be Stamped by the said Register, or his Deputy, or Deputies, upon the penalty of Forfeiting Ten pounds for each Offence, to such Register, to be Recovered by such Register, thereby Injured, by Action of Debt, Bill, Plaint, or Information, wherein no Essoin shall be Allowed, or more then one Imparlance.

Provided always, And be it further Enacted, and Declared by the Authority aforesaid; That no person or persons, shall be obliged to pay more then one penny for each of such Bonds or Bills.

And be it further Enacted by the Authority aforesaid; That the Words used by the party or parties, Transferring of the said Bonds

or

or Bills, shall be these, or to the like Effect following; That is to say,

I A. B. do Transfer this *Bill* to *C. D.* as Witness my Hand, this day of *Anno Domini*

And in Case there be Two or more Obligees, then the said Transferrer shall be in their Names, with proper Words to the Effect and Purport aforesaid, Mutatis Mutandis.

And be it further Enacted by the Authority aforesaid, That if any person or persons stand Indebted by such Bond or Bill, Acknowledged and Entred, as aforesaid, and shall refuse to pay such Debt or Debts, at the time the same shall become Due and Payable; Or at any time afterwards, such Creditor or Creditors, making Oath, that the Money Due thereon, hath been Demanded, and the Bond or Bill, Tendred to the party or parties Indebted, his, or their Executors, or Administrators, at his, or their, place or places of Aboad, or Residence, the said Oath to be made before the Justices of the Peace, at the Quarter Sessions, to be holden for the County, County of a City, or County of a Town, where the said Bond, or Bill, is Entred in open Court, between the Hours of Nine and Twelve in the Morning; Which Oath, the said Justices of the Peace, are hereby Impowered, and Required to Administer; and which Oath, the said Register, or his Deputy, are Required to Receive and Enter; then the said Register, or his Deputy, at the same Quarter-Sessions of the Peace, or at any other Quarter-Sessions to

be

be Holden for the said County, at any time within One Year after the said Money shall become due, and payable, upon the Delivery to him, the said Register, or his Deputy of the said Bond, or Bill, shall Issue a Warrant of Execution, under his Hand, and Seal of Office, Directed to all and every the High-Sheriffs, Coroners, Bailiffs, Seneschals, Stewards, and High-Constables of this Kingdom, against the person or persons, his or their Executors, or Administrators Owing the said Money, or his and their Goods and Chattles personal, for the Recovery, and Levying of the said Money, together with the Interest which shall then be Due; as also the Costs and Fees, for Entring of the said Bond or Bill, and for the Warrant of Execution, and other Fees, according to the Directions and Limitations, herein-after mentioned and expressed.

And to the end, all Disputes and Controversies, for, and concerning the Payment, and Discharge of such Debt or Debts, for, or on Account of such Bonds or Bills, may be prevented.

Be it further Enacted by the Authority aforesaid, That no Payment or Payments, shall be Esteemed, Valid, for, or on Account of such Bonds or Bills, unless the same be Entred on the back of the said Bond or Bill, by the party or parties, Interested therein, at the time of Entring of such Payment or Payments.

And be it further Enacted by the Authority aforesaid, That the Sheriffs, Coroners, Bailiffs, Seneschals, Stewards, and High-Constables, who shall have the Execution of the said Warrants, in their respective Counties, County

of

of a City, or County of a Town, Precincts and Liberties, shall have full Power and Authority, upon the Delivery of such Warrant or Warrants, to them respectively; and are accordingly hereby required to Arrest, and take the Body or Bodies, of the Person or Persons, against whom the said Warrants of Execution shall Issue, if so be the Party or Parties, Plantiff or Plantiffs, his, or their Servant, or Agent, shall desire the same: And in Case any Person or Persons, at such desire, shall be so Arrested or Taken, by any of the aforesaid Officers, appointed by this Act, who have not the Custody, or Keeping of Prisoners upon Execution, out of his Majesty's Four Courts, that then the Person or Persons so taken, shall be Delivered to the Plantiff, or his Servant, or Agent, to be carryed, and conveyed to the Sheriff, or other Officer, having the Custody of the Goal of the said County, where the said Person or Persons shall be so Taken, at the Charge and Peril of the said Plantiff; Who is hereby required to Receive and Keep, him or them, in safe Custody; Which said Sheriff, or other Officer, having the Custody of the said Goal, shall be chargable with the said Debtor or Debtors, in like manner, as if such Debtor or Debtors, had been taken upon a Capias ad Satisfaciendum, upon a Judgment at Common Law.

And be it further Enacted by the Authority aforesaid, That the said several Sheriffs, Coroners, Bailiffs, Seneschals, Stewards, and High-Constables in their respective Limits and Precincts, shall by the Authority of this Act, have full Power and Authority

thority upon such Warrant of Execution, against any person or persons Goods, at the desire of the party, or parties, Plantiff, or Plantiffs, his, or their Agent or Servant, to Seize and take the said person, or persons, Goods, and Chattles personal, in Execution, and the same to Appraise by the Appraisers of the Parish, or Barony, where the same shall be so taken or Seized, and shall give the Debtor, or Debtors if so be he, or they may be found, the First Refusal of the said Goods and Chattles personal, at the Appraised Rate; which if the said Debtor, or Debtors, shall refuse, or neglect to pay within Ten days after such Appraisement, then the said Goods and Chattles personal, shall be sold and delivered to the Plantiff, his Servant, or Agent, he, or they paying according to the Appraised Values, to the party or parties Interested, whatsoever Summ or Summs of Money the same shall amount unto, over and above the said Principal Debt, Interest, and Costs, according to the true intent and meaning of this Act, and for which, the said Warrant of Execution, shall be a sufficient Authority to the said Sheriff, Coroner, Bailiff, Seneschal, Steward, and High-Constable, and to every, or any of them, and that the said Sheriff, Coroner Bailiff, Seneschal, Steward, or High-Constable, shall make return thereon, in what manner the said Warrant was Executed, to the Register of the County, or his Deputy, or Deputies, from whence the said Warrant of Execution Issue, at, or before the next Quarter-Sessions of the Peace, to be holden for the said County, after such Execution Executed; which Warrant of Execution, with the

Reuern

Return thereof, shall be read in the open Court, and there Filed, and kept by the said Register, or his Deputy, and in case the Sheriff, or any other Officer, as aforesaid, appointed by this Act, shall on any such Warrant of Execution, take any person or persons, or his, or their Goods, or Chattles personal, in pursuance, or by Colour of this Act, and shall refuse, or neglect to execute, or make return of such Warrant of Execution in reasonable time, after the delivery thereof, and according to the Direction of this Act, upon reasonable demand made by the Plantiff or Plantiffs, his, or their Servant, or Agent, that then such Sheriff, or other Officer, as aforesaid, refusing, or neglecting so to do, shall be lyable to an Action on the Case, at the Sute of the said Plantiff, or Plantiffs, his, or their Executors, or Administrators, in like manner, as if the same had been an Execution, Executed on any Judgment at Law, either upon the Body, or Goods; and shall pay Treble Costs, in case Judgment shall pass for such Plantiff, or Plantiffs, his, or their Executors or Administrators.

Provided always, and be it further Enacted and Declared, by the Authority aforesaid, That all and every person, or persons, Plantiff, or Plantiffs in every such Warrant of Execution, shall from time to time, and at all times before such Execution, made and Executed, be at full Power and Liberty to make his Election or Choice, whether he will have the Body or Bodies, or Goods personal, taken in Execution, of the party, or parties, Defendant on such Warrant of Execution, as aforesaid; And that the said Sheriff, Coroner, Baliff,

Seneschal, Steward, and High-Constable, and every of them, shall pursue the Direction of the Plantiff, or Plantiffs, his, or their Servant, or Agent therein; and in Case the Plantiff, or Plantiffs, his or their Servant, or Agent, shall procure the said Defendants Body to be taken in Execution, then no further Execution on the Defendants Goods, shall be during the continuance of the said Defendants Imprisonment; or in Case the Plantiff, or Plantiffs; his or their Servant, or Agent, shall procure such Defendants Goods and Chattles personal, to be taken in Execution, which on Appraisment shall appear to be sufficient to answer the said Complainants Debt, Principal, Interest, and the Costs herein-after allowed; that then, no Execution shall be made on the said Defendants person, any thing herein contained to the contrary in any wise notwithstanding.

And be it further Enacted by the Authority aforesaid, That it shall, and may be Lawful, to, and for such person or persons, to whom any Money shall be Due, or Owing by such Bond or Bill, upon the back of such Bond, or Bill, in manner, as is aforesaid directed to Transfer, or Assign the Money so Due and Owing, together, with the Interest then accrued, or to accrue, and the Costs paid in pursuance, or according to the Direction of this Act, to any other person or persons whatsoever; and the same so Assigned, or Transferred, such Assignee or Assignes, his, or their Executors, or Administrators, shall have the Entire, and sole Right, Interest, and Property in the said Bond or Bill, together with the Money, Principal, Interest, and Costs due thereon,

Exclusively

Exclusively of any Right, Property, or Interest of any other person or persons, his, or their Executors, or Administrators, to whom the same was formerly Entred into, or Transferred, or Assigned, and that no Release, or Discharge of any such former Proprietor, after such Assignment, or Transferring, as aforesaid, shall any way operate to the Prejudice, or Damage of the party or parties, to whom the same shall be, as aforesaid, Assigned, or Transferred: but that the Assignee or Transferee, Assignes or Transferees, his, or their Executors, Administrators, or Assignes, who have, or hath the Right, or Interest in the said Bond or Bill, shall have the Warrant of Execution in his, or their own Name or Names, in as large, ample and beneficial manner, as if the said Bond or Bill, had been at first made to him or them; any Law, or Custom to the contrary notwithstanding.

Provided always, That the Transferring, or Assigning of such Bond or Bill, shall not any way Extend, or be Construed to Extend, to oblidge the person or persons, or Goods and Chattles of the party, or parties so Transferring, any thing in this Act, or any other Custom or Law, to the contrary hereof in anywise notwithstanding.

And be it further Enacted by the Authority aforesaid, That in case any person or persons, shall presume to Forge, or Counterfeit any Justice of the Peace's Hand or Seal, to any such Bond or Bill, or the Hand and Seal, of Office, of any such Register, or his Deputy or Deputies, to any such Warrant of Execution, or to any Indorsments, by such Register, or his Deputy

Deputy, or Deputies made, Certifying that such Bond, or Bill, was Registred according to, or in Pursuance of this Act, such person or persons so Offending, and thereof duly Convict, shall suffer such Pains, Penalties and Forfeitures, as a Felon, Without Benefit of Clergy.

And for the better preventing of all Partial, and Unfair Practices, by any Sheriff, Coroner, Bailiff, Seneschal, Steward, or High-Constable, in the Execution of this Act, or any part thereof.

Be it Enacted by the Authority aforesaid, That it shall, and may be lawful, to and for the Justices of Assize in their several Circuits, and Ridings, at their General Assizes, and to, and for the Justices of the Peace, at their General Quarter-Sessions, in their respective Counties, where such Partial, or Unfair Practices, shall be by them, or any of them committed, or done: and they are respectively hereby required, upon complaint thereof, to cause the party or parties Offending, as aforesaid to be thereof Indicted; and in case the party Offending, shall not submit, he shall be with all reasonable speed Tried, and if Verdict shall pass against him, or in case he shall submit, that then the Judge, or Judges of Assize, or Justices of the Peace, or Major part of them, shall, and may, by the Authority of this Act, and are hereby required to lay such Fine as to them respectively shall seem meet, and reasonable, not exceeding Ten pounds, the same to be Levyed within Thirty days after such Fine Imposed by Warrant of the said Court respectively, where the said complaint shall be made, upon the Goods of the person so Offending, and Convict, as aforesaid, without further Appeal, or Sute, in Law or Equity.

Provided

Provided always, That in Case the person so Offending, shall within the said Thirty days, make Satisfaction to the party or parties grieved, and shall procure his, or their Certificate, under his, or their Hands and Seals, to that Effect and Purpose, to the Clerk of the Crown, or Clerk of the Peace, respectively Directed, who is to Issue such Warrant, as aforesaid; that then, and in such Case, the said Clerk of the Crown, or Clerk of the Peace, respectively Directed, who is to Issue such Warrant, as aforesaid; that then, and in such Case, the said Clerk of the Crown, or Clerk of the Peace respectively, are hereby required to make stay of such Warrants, till the next Assizes, or next Quarter-Sessions respectively; at which time it shall, and may be lawful, to, and for the Judge or Judges of Assize, or Justices of the Peace, or major part of them, upon application to them respectively, at their General Assizes, or General Quarter-Sessions in open Court, the party or parties injured, being first satisfied, as aforesaid, to reduce such Fine or Fines, according to his, or their respective Discretion or Discretions.

And be it further Enacted by the Authority aforesaid, That in Case any person or persons, as aforesaid, Taken in Execution by any such Warrant of Execution in pursuance of this Act, shall Dye in Execution, the Debt shall not be Discharged thereby, but be lyable to be Levied, and Raised in manner as aforesaid, by Warrant of Execution, upon his, or their Goods and Chattles personal, wherever they may be found in this Kingdom. And to the end, Exaction, or Extortion of Fees for, or concerning the Execution of this Act, may be prevented.

Be it further Enacted by the Authority aforesaid, That the Register's Fees, for Entring the said Bond or Bill, and Certifying the same, shall be Six pence, and no more; And for Issuing a Warrant of Execution, One shilling, and no more; And for Entring of a Discharge of the said Bond or Bill, Three pence, and no more; And for Entring each Transfer, if desired, Two pence and no more; And that the Fees of the said Sheriff, Coroner, Bailiff Seneschal, Steward, or High-Constable, for the taking of the said Obligor, or for taking of his Goods and Chattles on the said Warrant of Execution, shall be One Shilling, and no more; and to the Appraiser, or Appraisers of such Goods and Chattles personal, Six pence in the pound, and no more; And to such Officer, or Officers, to whom the Custody of the said person in Execution shall be Committed, Six pence in the pound, and no more.

And be it further Enacted by the Authority aforesaid, That in Case any person or persons, shall corruptly take, or make any False Oath, or Suborn, or Procure any person or persons, corruptly to make such False Oath, for any matter, or thing relating to this Act, such person or persons, corruptly making such False Oath, or procuring such False Oath, corruptly to be made, being thereof Lawfully Convict, shall for every such Offence, Incur and Suffer, such, and the like pains and penalties, as are mentioned and prescribed, to be inflicted on persons Offending in Cases of Perjury, and Subornation, by one Act made in this Kingdom, in the Eighteenth year of the Reign of the late Queen Elizabeth of ever Glorious Memory, Intituled, An Act concerning willful Perjury.

And for preventing of the Abuses or Irregular Proceedings which may be otherwise committed or done by Registers, or their Deputies in the Execution of this Act.

Be it Enacted by the Authority aforesaid, That every Register, or his Deputy, or Deputies, of any County, or County of a City, or County of a Town, within this Kingdom, shall, and are hereby required, to deliver to the Clerk of the Peace, at every Quarter-Sessions, and to the Justice of the Peace, who is Chairman at such Quarter-Sessions, and to each of them, a Book fairly drawn, and Signed by such Register, or his Deputy, which shall be a true Copy of all Entries made since the former Sessions; in which Books, the said Clerk of the Peace, and Justice of the Peace, shall enter respectively, such Rules, Orders, and Proceedings, as shall be made at that Quarter-Sessions, and in open Court, shall cause the said Register to read over his Book, comparing it with the said Clerk of the Peace's Book, and the said Justice's Book, and making them all to agree; which being done, the said Justice of the Peace, Register, or his Deputy, and the Clerk of the Peace, shall all of them in open Court, in the presence of the Justices, composing the said Court, Sign their respective Names in each Book, and then the said Justices of the Peace, shall keep one of them, the Register another, and the Clerk of the Peace the third, which said Books, or two of them at least, shall be from Session to Session, brought into Court by the respective persons aforesaid.

FINIS.

www.ingramcontent.com/pod-product-compliance
Lightning Source LLC
Chambersburg PA
CBHW031812090426
42739CB00008B/1248
9783337148775